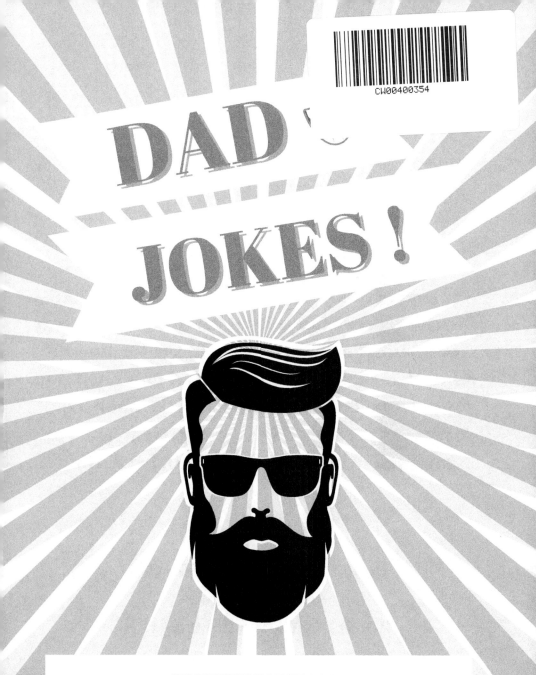

DAD JOKES !

THE BEST "WORST" JOKES & PUNS

Inspired by Jamie Raspin

Book Cover by Richard Atkin

Illustrations by Richard Atkin

Edition 1 2023

"What did the janitor say when he jumped out of the closet?"

"Supplies!"

"What did one wall say to the other?"

"I'll meet you at the corner."

I don't trust stairs.

They're always up to something."

"I used to hate faciial hair"
"then it grew on me"

A t-shirt and a vest get into a fight,

the vest shouts "dont hit me im armless"

"I used to be addicted to soap,

but I'm clean now."

"You think swimming with dolphins is expensive?

Swimming with sharks cost me an arm and a leg."

"Do you wanna box for your leftovers?"

"No, but I'll wrestle you for them."

"What country's capital is growing the fastest?"

"Ireland. Every day it's Dublin."

"I once had a dream I was floating in an ocean of orange soda.

It was more of a fanta sea."

"Why did the scarecrow win an award?

Because he was outstanding in his field."

"I'm reading a book about anti-gravity.

It's impossible to put down!"

"I've got a great joke about construction,

but I'm still working on it."

"Mountains aren't just funny.

They're hill areas."

"Why is Peter Pan always flying?"

"He neverlands."

"I could tell a joke about pizza,

but it's a little cheesy."

"What did the fish say when he hit the wall?

Dam."

To whoever stole my copy of Microsoft Office,

I will find you. You have my Word!

Two goldfish are in a tank. One says to the other,

"do you know how to drive this thing?"

My friend keeps saying "cheer up man it could be worse, you could be stuck underground in a hole full of water."

I know he means well.

I just watched a program about beavers.

It was the best dam program I've ever seen.

Two cannibals are eating a clown. One says to the other:

"Does this taste funny to you?"

What do you call a man who can't stand?

Neil.

Do you think glass coffins will be a success?

Remains to be seen.

I went to see my doctor this morning and told him "The tablets you gave me to stop me shrinking aren't working".

He said, "You'll just have to be a little patient."

It's a 5 minute walk from my house to the bar, but a 45 minute walk from the bar to my house...

The difference is staggering.

My wife said, "You really have no sense of direction, do you?"

I said, "Where did that come from?"

I met my boyfriend while visiting the zoo. There he was, in his uniform...

Straightaway I knew he was a keeper.

I tried to organize a professional Hide and Seek tournament, but it was a complete failure.

Good players are hard to find.

My wife screamed, "You haven't listened to a single word I've said, have you?!"

What a weird way to start a conversation.

My wife kicked me out because of my terrible Arnold Schwarzenegger impressions,

but don't worry. I'll return.

My wife traumatically ripped the blankets off me last night.

But I will recover.

I asked my date to meet me at the gym but she never showed up.

I guess the two of us aren't going to work out.

I can't believe there are 364 days left until Christmas...

And people have already got their decorations up.

I got a universal remote for Christmas.

This changes everything.

Today my kids told me they want a pony for Christmas.

I normally cook a turkey, but whatever makes them happy.

What do you call a row of men waiting for a hair cut?

A barbercue.

My wife threatened to divorce me when I said I was going to give our daughter a silly name.

So I called her Bluff.

If you ever get locked out of your house, talk to your lock calmly because...

Communication is key.

I always knock on the fridge door before I open it.

Just in case there's a salad dressing.

I caught my son chewing on electrical cords.

So I had to ground him.

My dad died when we couldn't remember his blood type.
As he died,

he kept insisting "be positive", but it's hard without him.

I've dedicated my whole life to finding a cure for insomnia.

I won't rest until I find it.

I've been prescribed
anti-gloating cream.

I can't wait to rub it in.

I accidentally drank a bottle of invisible ink last night.

I'm in the Hospital now, waiting to be seen.

Last weekend I got booed by my family and friends because I lit my fireworks in the wrong sequence! ...

Bang out of order.

I was wondering why the frisbee kept looking bigger and bigger,

and then it hit me.

It takes guts to be an organ donor.

I'm afraid for the calendar.

Its days are numbered.

To the person who stole my place in the queue.

I'm after you now.

Did you hear about the restaurant on the moon?

Great food, no atmosphere.

What did the slow tomato say to the others?

Don't worry I'll ketchup.

What do you call a pony with a sore throat?

A little hoarse.

What do you call cheese that isn't yours?

Nacho Cheese.

What's red and smells like blue paint?

Red paint.

How many tickles does it take to make an octopus laugh?

Ten tickles.

Why do Dads take an extra pair of socks when they go golfing?

In case they get a hole in one.

What did the ocean say to the beach?

Nothing, it just waved.

My wife asked me to stop singing 'Wonderwall' to her.

I said "Maybe...".

My dream job is to clean mirrors,

because I can really see myself doing that.

RIP, boiling water.

You will be mist.

Mom said I should do lunges to stay in shape.

That would be a big step forward.

I finally watched that documentary on clocks.

It was about time.

I have a joke about immortality,

and it never gets old.

To the person who stole my glasses:

I will find you. I have contacts.

To the person who stole my bed:

I won't rest until I find you.

To the person who stole my depression medication:

I hope you're happy now.

To the person who stole my case of energy drinks:

I hope you can't sleep at night.

Did you hear about the alligators that joined the FBI?

They became investigators.

The job of a scarecrow is a tough one

but hay... its in their jeans

Why did the man fall down the well?

Because he didn't see that well

Someone has glued my pack of cards together -

I don't know how to deal with it

What did the daddy buffalo say to his son when he left for work?

Bison

I went for an interview. They said, "Can you perform under pressure?"

I said "I'm not sure about that but I can have a good crack at Bohemian Rhapsody"

Why can't Elsa be trusted to hold a balloon?

Because she'll "Let it Go!"

What's the best part about living in Switzerland?

I don't know, but the flag is a big plus.

Oh no... I've just ordered 1000 litres of Tippex...

Big mistake.

My pet mouse Elvis died last night,

"he was caught in a trap!"

Just quit my job at the Helium factory.

I won't be spoken to in that tone!

Just adopted a dog from the local blacksmith,

soon as I got him home he made a bolt for the door.

"Dad, can you tell me what a solar eclipse is?"

No sun.

I am giving up drinking for a month. Sorry that came out wrong.

I am giving up. Drinking for a month.

I went to buy some camouflage pants the other day

but I couldn't find any.

My wife told me to pick up 8 cans of sprite at the grocery store

When I got home, I realized I only picked 7Up

I just found out I'm colour blind

"The news came out of the purple"

Two years ago my doctor told me I was going deaf

I haven't heard from him since

The guy who stole my iPad should Face time

What do you say to your sister when she's crying?

Are you having a crisis?

My girlfriend broke up with me because I'm a compulsive gambler. Ever since,

all I can think of is how to win her back.

What do you call a boomerang that won't come back?

A stick.

I got arrested for downloading the whole Wikipedia.

I told them I could explain everything.

My wife and I had a huge argument about who will do the laundry.

Eventually, I folded.

My hotel tried to charge me ten dollars extra for air conditioning.

That wasn't cool.

This graveyard looks overcrowded.

People must be dying to get in.

My son just said to me that he doesn't understand cloning. I said,

"That makes two of us".

There's been an explosion at a cheese factory in Paris.

There's nothing left but de Brie.

My wife says she's leaving me because she thinks I'm too obsessed with astronomy.

What planet is she on!

I tried to have a conversation with my wife when she was applying a mud pack.

You should have seen the filthy look she gave me.

What do you call a woman who sounds like an ambulance?

Nina.

My mum bought me a really cheap dictionary for my birthday.

I couldn't find the words to thank her.

Printed in Great Britain
by Amazon